1 MONTH OF
FREE
READING

at

www.ForgottenBooks.com

By purchasing this book you are eligible for one month membership to ForgottenBooks.com, giving you unlimited access to our entire collection of over 1,000,000 titles via our web site and mobile apps.

To claim your free month visit:

www.forgottenbooks.com/free233372

ISBN 978-0-265-22094-8
PIBN 10233372

THE

CHRONOLOGY OF THE BIBLE.

By SAMUEL SHARPE,

AUTHOR OF "THE HISTORY OF EGYPT"

— ———

LONDON:

J. RUSSELL SMITH, 36, SOHO SQUARE.

—

1868.

LONDON:
PRINTED BY WOODFALL AND KINDER,
MILFORD LANE, STRAND, W.C.

5851
25/9/90

PREFACE.

VERY few words are needed to show the importance of Chronology. The moral teachings of History may gain our warmer admiration, but Chronology is the skeleton or framework which supports the several parts of History, and saves the whole from falling into a confused heap. The Hebrew Chronology, in particular, has many claims on our notice; first, for its help towards our understanding the Bible; and, secondly, for its contribution towards the Chronology of the neighbouring nations, particularly of Egypt and Assyria.

The Chronology of the ancient world is indebted first to Babylon for its recorded eclipses, preserved for us by Claudius Ptolemy the Astronomer, and then to those countries that were ruled by a succession of monarchs, whose reigns measured time with a convenience unknown to their republican neighbours. Were all modern and intermediate Chronology destroyed, or any number of links in the chain broken between the present time and the overthrow of the

Persian monarchy by Alexander the Great, yet our knowledge of the previous dates would remain unchanged. The moon's place as determined by an eclipse or by the occultation of a star is an independent event, which, when recorded with its day and hour, and year of a king's reign, enables an astronomer to fix by his calculations that otherwise unknown time with the same mathematical certainty that a sailor fixes his unknown place in longitude on the ocean. Thus the Babylonian eclipses give us a fixed point from which we may measure time. And the unbroken time of Jewish kings following one another in quiet succession, from father to son, reaching over a period of four hundred years from Solomon to Zedekiah, who all dated by the years of their reigns, carries our reckoning back with reasonable certainty from the time of these eclipses at Babylon to the tenth century before the Christian era. It thus fixes the time of Solomon's reign, from which, as from a new starting point, the history of the world must be traced backwards along the line of Egyptian kings. The history of the Israelites under their Judges has come down to us in a form too broken to be of much chronological value; and the succession of patriarchs before the time of the Judges can have no claim to attention as a portion of History.

But the History, and therefore the Chronology, of the Hebrew monarchy deserve at least as much attention as they receive. During that time were written the most valuable of the Hebrew books. Perhaps the Book of Judges alone was written before the rise of the monarchy; and only the less valuable portions of the other books were written after its fall. The laws in the Pentateuch, when they are ecclesiastical, are also political; the Psalms are as much political as devotional; the writings of the Prophets are wholly political, though dictated by religious zeal and clothed in a religious dress; and all these, to be properly understood, must have their place in History assigned, by noting what political events give rise to the laws or are spoken of as contemporaneous with the writer. Hence any service that Chronology renders to the History is a service rendered to the religious portions of the Bible.

WORKS BY THE SAME AUTHOR.

THE NEW TESTAMENT, translated from Griesbach's Text. Fifth Edition.

THE HEBREW SCRIPTURES TRANSLATED ; being a Revision of the Authorized English Old Testament. In 3 vols

TEXTS FROM THE HOLY BIBLE, explained by the help of the Ancient Monuments.

HISTORIC NOTES ON THE BOOKS OF THE OLD AND NEW TESTAMENTS. Second Edition.

CRITICAL NOTES ON THE AUTHORIZED ENGLISH VERSION OF THE NEW TESTAMENT. Second Edition.

THE HISTORY OF EGYPT, from the Earliest Times till the Conquest by the Arabs, in A.D. 640. Fourth Edition.

THE CHRONOLOGY AND GEOGRAPHY OF ANCIENT EGYPT.

ALEXANDRIAN CHRONOLOGY.

EGYPTIAN INSCRIPTIONS, from the British Museum and other sources. 216 Plates, in Folio.

EGYPTIAN HIEROGLYPHICS ; being an Attempt to Explain their Nature, Origin, and Meaning. With a Vocabulary.

EGYPTIAN ANTIQUITIES IN THE BRITISH MUSEUM described.

EGYPTIAN MYTHOLOGY AND EGYPTIAN CHRISTIANITY, with their Influence on the Opinions of Modern Christianity.

TABLE OF CONTENTS.

THE CHRONOLOGY OF THE BIBLE.

INTRODUCTION.

In this work the writer ventures on no opinion about the age of the world, or the number of years that it has been inhabited by man, nor even attempts to decide the date of the Exodus of the Israelites out of Egypt, under Moses. His aim is merely to show at what times the Hebrew writers place those events. He has simply taken out the spaces of time mentioned in the Bible, and placed them together in a series till they come down to the recorded eclipses. Modern science tells us with certainty how many years before our own time these eclipses happened; and thus to the Table of years which had been made by counting forward, we are able to put our own more usual and more convenient dates by counting backwards, from the Christian era. Thus, if an eclipse is known to have taken place 2489 years before this present year, which we call 1868, we deduct 1868 from the above number, and say that it happened B.C. 621.

The chronology of the Old Testament may conveniently be divided into two parts, the traditional chronology and the historical chronology.

The first is formed by adding together the age of each of the patriarchs at the time of the son's birth, from which we learn that Abraham left Haran in Syria in A.M. 2023 ; that the Exodus of the Israelites from Egypt took place in A.M. 2668; and that Solomon, in the fourth year of his reign, built the Temple of Jerusalem in A.M. 3148. Here the traditional chronology may be said to end; and, after this time, the dates are recorded with so much greater care, and with such an evident aim at exactness, that we may safely consider that we have entered upon historical chronology. From this we learn that the building of the Temple took place in the year B.C. 973. We thus gain the opinion of the Hebrew writers that Adam was created in the year B.C. 4121 (= 3148 + 973).

The received chronology places the creation of Adam in the year B.C. 4004, or 4000 years before the birth of Jesus; and it will be not uninteresting to examine the reasons for its doing so. The Epistle of Barnabas mentions an opinion held by the Jews, that the world was to be destroyed at the end of 6000 years from its creation, because, according to Genesis chap. i., it was created in six days, and, according to 2 Peter iii. 8, "one day with the Lord is as a thousand years." On comparing this with our chronology, it will be seen that the Promises were given to Abraham in A.M. 2023, and that Jesus was born in A.M. 4121. Hence, a very little alteration of the dates will make the Bible seem to declare that mankind had lived 2000 years before the Promises, 2000 more before the Gospel; and this adjustment of the chronology, to make it agree with a fanciful opinion, has been made in the margin of the authorized English Bibles. This opinion also led to the natural prophecy, among those who are fond of such fanciful interpretations, that the world is to last 2000 years under the Gospel, and to come to an end in A.D. 2000, or more exactly, in A.D. 1996, because modern criticism has made it probable that Jesus was born in the year B.C. 4.

TABLE OF THE TRADITIONAL CHRONOLOGY FROM THE CREATION TO SOLOMON'S REIGN.

GENESIS.								A.M.
V. 3	Adam,	when	130	years old,	begat	Seth	. .	130
6	Seth,	,,	105	,,	,,	,, Enos	. .	235
9	Enos,	,,	90	,,	,,	,, Cainan	.	325
12	Cainan,	,,	70	,,	,,	,, Mahalaleel		395
15	Mahalaleel,	,,	65	,,	,,	,, Jared	. .	460
18	Jared,	,,	162	,,	,,	,, Enoch	. .	622
21	Enoch,	,,	65	,,	,,	,, Methuselah		687
25	Methuselah,	,,	187	,,	,,	,, Lamech	.	874
28	Lamech,	,,	182	,,	,,	,, Noah	. .	1056
32	Noah,	,,	500	,,	,,	,, Shem	. .	1556
VII. 6	,,	,,	600	,,	,,	The Flood	. .	1656
XI. 10	Two years after the Flood, Shem begat Arphaxad .							1658
12	Arphaxad,	when	35	years old,	,,	Salah	. .	1693
14	Salah,	,,	30	,,	,,	,, Eber	. .	1723
16	Eber,	,,	34	,,	,,	,, Peleg	. .	1757
18	Peleg,	,,	30	,,	,,	,, Reu	. .	1787
20	Reu,	,,	32	,,	,,	,, Serug	. .	1819
22	Serug,	,,	30	,,	,,	,, Nahor	. .	1849
24	Nahor,	,,	29	,,	,,	,, Terah	. .	1878
26	Terah,	,,	70	,,	,,	,, Abram	. .	1948
XII. 4	Abram,	,,	75	,,	,,	left Haran	. .	2023
XXI. 5	When 100 years old, 25 years later, begat Isaac . . .							2048
XXV. 26	Isaac,	when	60	years old,	,,	Jacob	. .	2108
XLVII. 9	Jacob,	,,	130	,,	,,	settles in Egypt .		2238
EXODUS.								
XII. 40	After 430 years, they leave Egypt							2668
1 KINGS.								
VI. 1	480 years after the Exodus is the 4th of Solomon .							3148

ON THE BOOK OF JUDGES.

THE above-mentioned period of 480 years, which the
writer of 1 Kings vi. 1, places between the Exodus
and the building of the Temple by Solomon, would
seem to have been learned by adding together the
times mentioned in the history. In the Books of
Joshua and Judges there are periods amounting to
460 years. If we continue, in the same way, to think
none of the events contemporaneous, we must add
to this sum,—

 1 year from the Exodus to the espying of the
  land.—Numb. x. 11.—xiii. 2.
 40 years of David's reign.
 3 years of Solomon's reign to the building of the
  Temple ;

making a total of 504 years. How the writer les-
sened this down to 480 it is in vain to conjecture.
Sound criticism would lead us to lessen it much more
by considering many events in the Book of Judges
as contemporaneous.

 Thus, in chapters vi.—xii. we have a continuous
history, limited for the most part to the middle
tribes of Ephraim and Manasseh, though sometimes we find Gad, Issachar, and Zebulun joined to
them. This describes an invasion and conquest of
their country by the Midianites and others from the
east of the Jordan, and then the reigns of Gideon
and Abimelech, and the judgeships of Tola and Jair
(chap. x. 1, 4). These quiet reigns are followed by

a second great invasion and conquest of the land.
This is by the children of Ammon from the east,
and by the Philistines from the south, and it is followed by the judgeships of Jephthah, Ibzan, Elon,
and Abdon. The whole occupies 144 years; namely,
95 years before the second invasion, and 49 years
after it. It seems probable that these two portions
embrace the whole period of time which the Book of
Judges covers, and that the other invasions relate to
other parts of the, country which sometimes had
judges of their own. Thus the wars of Benjamin
against the Moabites, and the conquest of Moab, in
chap. iii. 14—30, and the wars of the northern tribes
against the Syrians, in chap. iii. 8—11, and against
the Canaanites, in chap. iv, v., may have taken place
during the first of these periods; and Samson's wars
against the Philistines, in chap. xiii—xvi., may have
been included in the second period of time. This
shortening of the chronology of this book will make
it better agree with the genealogies; for, since Moses
is the fourth in descent from Jacob, and David the
eleventh, we cannot allow more than four, or at
most five, generations of men to the time occupied
by the Book of Judges.

On the other hand, the Book of Judges, in chap.
xi. 26, has preserved a tradition, relating to a yet
earlier time, that the Israelites had dwelt for 300
years on the east of the Jordan, between the time
of the Exodus and the time of Judges ruling in
Canaan. This very probable statement is expressly
contradicted in Numb. xxxii. 12, xxxiv. 17, and
Joshua iii.

THE CHRONOLOGY OF THE SEPTUAGINT.

WHEN the Greek Jews made the Septuagint version, in the reign of Ptolemy Philadelphus, they seem not to have been content with the very moderate antiquity for their nation and the human race given in the Hebrew books; and, accordingly, they added 1466 years to the age of the world, by making the patriarchs older at the birth of their sons. They thus add 586 in Genesis v.—vii., and 880 in Genesis xi., xii. They probably meant to add an exact Egyptian cycle of four times 365, or 1460 years. The difference of six years may be an error of the scribe. On comparing the Greek chronology with the Hebrew, sound criticism will certainly lead us to conclude that the Hebrew is what the writers originally wrote. However mistaken we may think them in supposing that the world had only been peopled with mankind for such a small number of years, yet we cannot accept the Greek chronology as the original. It is evidently a correction, an attempted improvement on the Hebrew. And even as an improvement it is of very little value, since even with its help we by no means carry back the creation of man to a time early enough to satisfy the reasonable requirements of science.

A second improvement proposed by the Greek translators was to shorten the time of the Israelites' residence in Egypt—the time between Jacob's bringing his family into Egypt and Moses' leading them out. This, in the above table, is quoted from Exodus xii. 40, as 430 years. But in the Greek, this period of 430 years is said to include their residence in Canaan as well as their residence in Egypt, commencing with Abraham's leaving Haran; and it thus shortens the residence in Egypt by 215 years. This certainly agrees better with the genealogies; but it cannot be accepted as what the writer originally wrote.

THE SECOND OR HISTORICAL PORTION OF THE HEBREW CHRONOLOGY.

THIS is calculated backwards from the eclipse in the 5th of Nabopulassar, B.C. 621, by the help of the years mentioned in Ezekiel, Jeremiah, and the Books of Kings. In the Books of Kings we often meet with contradictory statements. The length of the reign, as there stated, does not always agree with the length as we should calculate it to be, when the writer gives us a date for its ending, and also a date for the end of the previous reign. The latter mode of determining the length seems to be of the two the more trustworthy. The contradiction can only be reconciled upon the supposition that many of the kings reigned jointly with their fathers, and had thus been nominally reigning several years before their real reign began. This is the supposition of many of the best Biblical critics. Our Table thus makes the reign of Solomon about thirty-nine years more modern than the received chronology, which, on the other hand, supposes each king of Judah to have counted his years from his father's death. Thus, with us, it

becomes unnecessary to place an interregnum between
Jeroboam II. of Israel and his son Zachariah, and
a second interregnum between Pekah of Israel and
Hosea who dethroned him.

The received chronology, which may be seen in the
margin of most Bibles, is formed by simply adding
up together the length of every king's reign, overlooking the difficulty caused by the double method
of reckoning employed in the Books of Kings, and
overlooking the fact, certain in some cases and probable in others, that a king's years were reckoned,
not from his father's death, but from when he was
associated with his father on the throne. If we had
nothing to guide us but the Books of Chronicles, we
should be driven to that mode of reasoning. But the
Books of Kings teach us otherwise, and thus lead us
to shorten the sum of the kings' reigns by thirty-nine
years.

When the reigns of the Jewish kings come to an
end, the Table is continued forwards by the help of
Claudius Ptolemy, to the seventh year of Cambyses,
which is again fixed by an eclipse; and to the second
year of Darius, when the Jews had leave to rebuild
the Temple.

The quotations from the historians, by which the
Table is formed, are placed at the end of it.

TABLE OF HEBREW CHRONOLOGY·

B.C.	JUDAH.	ISRAEL.
1016	David in Hebron [1]	Ish-bosheth or Ish-baal
1008	DAVID	
976	SOLOMON [2]	
936	1 of Rehoboam .	1 of Jeroboam .
935	2 . . .	2 . . . .
934	3 . . .	3 . . . .
933	4 . . .	4 . . . .
932	5 . . .	5 . . . .
931	6 . . .	6 . . . .
930	7 . . .	7 . . . .
929	8 . . .	8 . . . .
928	9 . . .	9 . . . .
927	10 } . .	10 . . . .
926	11 . . .	11 . . . .
925	12 . . .	12 . . . .
924	13 . . .	13 . . . .
923	14 . . .	14 . . . .
922	15 . . .	15 . . . .
921	16 . . .	16 . . . .
920	17 . . [3]	17 . . . .
919	(18) 1 of Abijam [4]	18 . . . .
918	(19) 2 . .	19 . . . .
917	(20) 3 . 1 of Asa [5]	20 . . . .
916	(21) 2 . . .	21 . 1 of Nadab [6]
915	(22) 3 . . .	22 . 2 . 1 of Baasha [7]
914	(23) 4 . . .	2 . . . .
913	(24) 5 . . .	3 . . . .
912	(25) 6 . . .	4 . . . .
911	(26) 7 . . .	5 . . . .

B.C.	JUDAH.	ISRAEL.
910	(27) 8 of Asa . . .	6 of Baasha . . .
909	(28) 9	7 . . . . .
908	(29) 10	8 . . . . .
907	(30) 11	9 . . . . .
906	(31) 12	10 . . . . .
905	(32) 13	11 . . . . .
904	(33) 14	12 . . . . .
903	(34) 15	13 . . . . .
902	(35) 16	14 . . . . .
901	(36) 17 . . [8]	15 . . . . .
900	18	16 . . . . .
899	19	17 . . . . .
898	20	18 . . . . .
897	21	19 . . . . .
896	22	20 . . . . .
895	23	21 . . . . .
894	24	22 . . . . .
893	25	23 . . . . .
892	26	24 . 1 of Elah . [9]
891	27	2 . 1 . 1 of Omri & Tibni
890	28	2 . 2 . . [10]
889	29	3 . 3 . . .
888	30	4 . 4 . . .
887	31	5 . 5 . . .
886	32	6 of Omri alone
885	33	7 . . . . .
884	34	8 . . . . .
883	35	9 . . . . .
882	36	10 . . . . .
881	37	11 . . . . .
880	38	12 . 1 of Ahab . [11]
879	39	2 . . . . .
878	40	3 . . . . .
877	41 . 1 of Jehoshaphat [12]	4 . . . . .
876	2	5 . . . . .
875	3	6 . . . . .
874	4	7 . . . . .
873	5	8 . . . . .
872	6	9 . . . . .
871	7	10 . . . . .

B.C.	JUDAH.	ISRAEL.
870	8 of Jehoshaphat .	11 of Abab . .
869	9	12 . . . .
868	10 . . .	13 . . . .
867	11	14 . . . .
866	12	15 . . . .
865	13	16 . . . .
864	14 . . .	17 . . . .
863	15	18 . . . .
862	16	19 . . . .
861	17	20.1 of Ahaziah [13]
860	18	21.2.1 of Jehoram [14]
859	19	22. 2 . . .
858	20	3 . . . .
857	21	4 . . . .
856	22 . 1 of Jehoram [15]	5 . . . .
855	23 . 2 . . .	6 . . . [16]
854	24 . 3 . . .	7 . . . .
853	25 . 4 . . .	8 . . . .
852	5	9 . . . .
851	6	10 . . . .
850	7	11 . . . .
849	{ 8 . 1 of Ahaziah [17] { 1 of Athaliah [19]	{ 12 . . . . { 1 of Jehu . [18]
848	2	2 . . . .
847	3	3 . . . .
846	4	4 . . . .
845	5	5 . . . .
844	6	6 . . . .
843	7 . 1 of Jehoash [20]	7 . . . .
842	2	8 . . . .
841	3	9 . . . .
840	4	10 . . . .
839	5	11 . . . .
838	6	12 . . . .
837	7	13 . . . .
836	8	14 . . . .
835	9	15 . . . .
834	10	16 . . . .
833	11	17 . . . .
832	12	18 . . . .
831	13	19 . . . .

B.C.	JUDAH.	ISRAEL.
830	14 of Jehoash . .	20 of Jehu . .
829	15	21 . . . .
828	16	22 . . . .
827	17	23 . . . .
826	18	24 . . . .
825	19	25 . . . .
824	20	26 . . . .
823	21	27 . . . .
822	22	28 . . . .
821	23	1 of Jehoahaz [21]
820	24	2 . . . .
819	25	3 . . . .
818	26	4 . . . .
817	27	5 . . . .
816	28	6 . . . .
815	29	7 . . . .
814	30	8 . . . .
813	31	9 . . . .
812	32	10 . . . .
811	33	11 . . . .
810	34	12 . . . .
809	35	13 . . . .
808	36	14 . . . .
807	37	15 . 1 of Jehoash [22]
806	38 . 1 of Amaziah [23]	16 . 2 . . .
805	39 . 2 . . .	17 . 3 . . .
804	40 . 3 . . .	4 . 1 of Jeroboam II.
803	4	5 . 2 jointly with his
802	5	6 . 3 father
801	6 . 1 Azariah, [25]	7 . 4 . . .
800	7 . 2 when 16 years	8 . 5 . . .
799	8 . 3 old, jointly with	9 . 6 . . .
798	9 . 4 his father .	10 . 7 . . .
797	10 . 5 . . .	11 . 8 . . .
796	11 . 6 . . .	12 . 9 . . .
795	12 . 7 . . .	13 . 10 . . .
794	13 . 8 . . .	14 . 11 . . .
793	14 . 9 . . .	15 . 12 . . .
792	15 . 10 . . .	16 . 13 Jeroboam II.
791	16 . 11 . . .	14 . . alone [24]

	JUDAH.	ISRAEL.
)	17 . 12 of Amaziah and	15 of Jeroboam II. .
)	18 . 13 Azariah.	16 . . . .
3	19 . 14 . . .	17 . . . .
7	20 . 15 . . .	18 . . . .
6	21 . 16 . . .	19 . . . .
5	22 . 17 . . .	20 . . . .
4	23 . 18 . . .	21 . . . .
3	24 . 19 . . .	22 . . . .
2	25 . 20 . . .	23 . . . .
1	26 . 21 . . .	24 . . . .
0	27 . 22 . . .	25 . . . .
9	28 . 23 . . .	26 . . . .
8	29 . 24 Azariah or Uz-	27 . . . .
7	25 . ziah alone [26]	28 . . . .
6	26	29 . . . .
5	27	30 . . . .
4	28	31 . . . .
3	29	32 . . . .
2	30	33 . . . .
1	31	34 . . . .
0	32	35 . . . .
9	33	36 . . . .
8	34	37 . . . .
7	35	38 . . . .
6	36	39 . . . .
5	37	40 . . . .
4	38	41 . 1 of Zachariah [27]
3	39 . . . {	1 of Shallum [28]
		1 of Menahem [29]
2	40	2 . . . .
1	41	3 . . . .
0	42	4 . . . .
9	43	5 . . . .
8	44	6 . . . .
7	45	7 . . . .
6	46	8 . . . .
5	47	9 . . . .
4	48	10 . . . .
3	49	(11?) . . [30]
2	50	1 of Pekahiah [31]
1	51	2 . . . .

c

B.C.	JUDAH.	ISRAEL.
750	52 of Azariah or Uzziah	1 of Pekah [32]
749	1 of Jotham [33]	2 . . . .
748	2	3 . . . .
747	3	4 . . . .
746	4	5 . . . .
745	5	6 . . . .
744	6	7 . . . .
743	7	8 . . . .
742	8	9 . . . .
741	9 . 1 of Ahaz . .	10 . . . .
740	10 . 2 . . .	11 . . . .
739	11 . 3 . . .	12 . . . .
738	12 . 4 . . .	13 . . . .
737	13 . 5 . . .	14 . . . .
736	14 . 6 . . .	15 . . . .
735	15 . 7 . . .	16 . . . .
734	16 . 8 . . [34]	17 . . . .
733	(17) . 9 . . .	18 . . . .
732	(18) .10 . . .	19 . . . .
731	(19) .11 . . .	20 . . . .
730	(20) .12 . . .	1 of Hoshea [35]
729	13	2 . . . .
728	14	3 . . . .
727	15 . 1 of Hezekiah [36]	4 . . . .
726	16 . 2 . . .	5 . . . .
725	3	6 . . . .
724	4 . . . [37]	7 . . . .
723	5	8 . . . .
722	6 . . [38]	9 Shalmanezer con-
721	7 . . [39]	quers Israel.
720	8	
719	9	
718	10	
717	11	
716	12	
715	13	
714	14	Sennacherib's overthrow.
713	15	Berodach Baladan's em-
712	16	[bassy.
711	17	

B.C.	JUDAH.				
710	18 of Hezekiah				.
709	19	.	.	.	.
708	20	.	.	.	.
707	21	.	.	.	.
706	22	.	.	.	.
705	23	.	.	.	.
704	24	.	.	.	.
703	25	.	.	.	.
702	26	.	.	.	.
701	27	.	.	.	.
700	28	.	.	.	.
399	29	.	.	.	.
398	1 of Manasseh			[40]	
397	2	.	.	.	.
396	3	.	.	.	.
395	4	.	.	.	.
394	5	.	.	.	.
393	6	.	.	.	.
92	7	.	.	.	.
91	8	.	.	.	.
90	9	.	.	.	.
89	10	.	.	.	.
88	11	.	.	.	.
87	12	.	.	.	.
86	13	.	.	.	.
85	14	.	.	.	.
84	15	.	.	.	.
83	16	.	.	.	.
82	17	.	.	.	.
81	18	.	.	.	.
80	19	.	.	.	.
79	20	.	.	.	.
78	21	.	.	.	.
77	22	.	.	.	.
76	23	.	.	.	.
75	24	.	.	.	.
74	25	.	.	.	.
73	26	.	.	.	.
72	27	.	.	.	.
71	28	.	.	.	.

At year 83: Esarhaddon succeeds Sennacherib.

B.C.	JUDAH.			
670	29 of Manasseh	.		.
669	30	.	.	.	.
668	31	.	.	.	.
667	32	.	.	.	.
666	33	.	.	.	.
665	34	.	.	.	.
664	35	.	.	.	.
663	36	.	.	.	.
662	37	.	.	.	.
661	38	.	.	.	.
660	39	.	.	.	.
659	40	.	.	.	.
658	41	.	.	.	.
657	42	.	.	.	.
656	43	.	.	.	.
655	44	.	.	.	.
654	45	.	.	.	.
653	46	.	.	.	.
652	47	.	.	.	.
651	48	.	.	.	.
650	49	.	.	.	.
649	50	.	.	.	.
648	51	.	.	.	.
647	52	.	.	.	.
646	53	.	.	.	.
645	54	.	.	.	.
644	55	.	.	.	.
643	1 of Amon	.	[41]
642	2	.	.	.	.
641	1 of Josiah	.	[42]
640	2	.	.	.	.
639	3	.	.	.	.
638	4	.	.	.	.
637	5	.	.	.	.
636	6	.	.	.	.
635	7	.	.	.	.
634	8	.	.	.	.
633	9	.	.	.	.
632	10	.	.	.	.
631	11	.	.	.	.

B.C.	JUDAH.	BABYLON.
630	12 of Josiah . .	
629	13 . . . [43]	
628	14 . . .	
627	15 . . .	
626	16 . . .	
625	17 . . . . '	1 of Nabopulassar .
624	18 . . .	2 . . .
623	19 . . .	3 . . .
622	20 . . .	4 . . . .
621	21 . . .	5 An eclipse recorded
620	22 . . .	6 . . . [44]
619	23 . . .	7 . . .
618	24 . . .	8 . . .
617	25 . . .	9 . . .
616	26 . . .	10 . . .
615	27 . . .	11 . . .
614	28 . . .	12 . . .
613	29 . . .	13 . . .
612	30 . . .	14 . . .
611	31 . . .	15 . . .
610	{ 1 of Jehoahaz } [45] { 1 of Jehoiakim }	16 . . .
609	2 . . .	17 . . .
608	3 . . .	18 . . .
607	4 . . . [46]	19 . 1 of Nebuchad-
606	5 . . .	20 . 2 . [nezzar
605	6 . . .	21 . 3 . .
604	7 . . .	22 . 4 . .
603	8 . . .	23 . 5 . .
602	9 . . .	24 . 6 . .
601	10 . [Captivity [47]	25 . 7 . .
600	11 . 1 of Jehoiachin or	26 . 8 . .
599	2 . 1 of Zedekiah [48]	27 . 9 . .
598	3 . 2 . .	28 . 10 . .
597	4 . 3 . .	29 . 11 . .
596	5 . 4 . .	30 . 12 . [49]
595	6 . 5 . .	31 . 13 . .
594	7 . 6 . .	32 . 14 . .
593	8 . 7 . .	33 . 15 . .
592	9 . 8 . .	34 . 16 . .
591	10 . 9 . .	35 . 17 . .

B.C.	JUDAH.		BABYLON.
590	11 of Captivity	10 of Zedekiah	18 of Nebuchad-
589	12 . .	11 . 1 of City	19 [nezzar [50]
588	13 . .	2 smitten[51]	20 „
587	14 . .	3 . .	21 „
586	15 . .	4 . .	22 „
585	16 . .	5 . .	23 „
584	17 . .	6 . .	24 „
583	18 . .	7 . .	25 „
582	19 . .	8 . .	26 „
581	20 . .	9 . .	27 „
580	21 . .	10 . .	28 „
579	22 . .	11 . .	29 „
578	23 . .	12 . .	30 „
577	24 . .	13 . .	31 „
576	25 . .	14 . [52]	32 „
575	26 . .	15 . .	33 „
574	27 . .	16 . .	34 „
573	28 . .	17 . .	35 „
572	29 . .	18 . .	36 . „
571	30 . .	19 . .	37 „
570	31 . .	20 . .	38 „
569	32 . .	21 . .	39 „
568	33 . .	22 . .	40 „
567	34 . .	23 . .	41 „
566	35 . .	24 . .	42 „
565	36 . .	25 . .	43 „
564	37 Jehoiachin	26 . .	44 . 1 of Evil [53]
563	released from	27 . .	45 . 2 Merodach
562	prison	28 . .	46 . 3 „
561		29 . .	47 . 4 „
560		30 . .	48 . 1 of Nerig-
559		31 . .	49 . 2 [lissor
558		32 . .	50 . 3 „
557		33 . .	51 . 4 „
556		34 . .	52 . 5 „
555		35 . .	53 . 1 of Na-[54]
554		36 . .	54 . 2 bonned or
553		37 . .	55 . 3 Belshazzar
552		38 . .	56 . 4 „
551		39 . .	57 . 5 „

B.C.	JUDAH.		BABYLON.	
550	40 of City smit-	58 of　Nebu-	6 of Nabon-	
549	41　　　[ten	59 chadnezzar	7 ned or Bel-	
548	42　.　.	60 or of Jere-	8 shazzar	
547	43　.　.	61 miah's pro-	9　　"	
546	44　.　.	62 phecy	10　"	
545	45　.　.	63　.　.	11　"	
544	46　.　.	64　.　.	12　"	
543	47　.　.	65　.　.	13　"	
542	48　.　.	66　.　.	14　"	
541	49　.　.	67　.　.	15　"	
540	50　.　.	68　.　.	16　"	
539	51　.　.	69　.　.	17　"	
538	52 Prince Ze-	70　.　[55]	1 of　Cyaxares	
537	53　　[rubbabel		2 II. or Darius	
536	54　.　.		3 the Mede and	
535	55　.　.		4 of　Cyrus in	
534	56　.　.		5 Babylon[56]	
533	57　.　.		6　　"	
532	58　.　.		7　　"	
531	59　.　.		8　　"	
530	60　.　.		9　　"	
529	61　.　.		1 of Cambyses	
528	62　.　.		2　　"	
527	63　.　.		3　　"	
526	64　.　.		4　　"	
525	65　.　.		5　　"	
524	66　.　.		6　　"	
523	67　.　.		7 An　eclipse	
522	68　.　.		8 recorded[57]	
521	69　.　.		1 of Darius	
520	70　.　.		2　　"　　[58]	
516	The Temple finished　.　.		6 of Darius [59]	
483	Esther made Queen of Persia		3 of Xerxes I. [60]	
479	Ezra returns to Jerusalem　.		7 of Xerxes I. [61]	
445	Nehemiah returns to Jerusalem		20 of　Artaxerxes [62]	

NOTES.

CONTAINING THE AUTHORITIES FOR THE FOREGOING
TABLE OF THE KINGS OF JUDAH, ISRAEL, AND
BABYLON.

————

(1.) DAVID reigned forty years, namely, seven years and six months in Hebron over Judah, and then in Jerusalem thirty-three years over both Israel and Judah; 2 Samuel v. 5.

(2.) Solomon reigned forty years over all Israel; 1 Kings xi. 42. Some small portion of this may have been jointly with his father David.

(3.) Rehoboam, the son of Solomon, reigned seventeen years over Judah; 1 Kings xiv. 21.

(4.) Abijam, the son of Rehoboam, began to reign in the eighteenth year of Jeroboam, and reigned three years over Judah; 1 Kings xv. 1.

To this reign, said to be of three years, we can only allow two; and the same dropping of a year will be observed in many other cases. This is explained in the Mishna, in treatise Rosh Hashanah, chap. i., where we read that the years of a king's reign were said to end with the New Year's day; and thus the first year of every reign may have consisted of only a few weeks or even a few days. The same, of course, was the case with the last year of a reign. Thus the last year of one king and the first of his successor together only filled twelve months. This mode of reckoning the regnal years was used throughout Egypt, Babylonia, Syria, and Asia Minor, even for the Greek kings and Roman emperors who afterwards reigned over those countries; and it will have to be attended to when we meet with authors who lived in those countries dating the baptism and crucifixion of Jesus by means of the years of an emperor's reign.

(5.) Asa, the son of Abijam, began to reign over Judah in the twentieth year of Jeroboam, and reigned forty-one years; 1 Kings xv. 9.

(6.) Nadab, the son of Jeroboam, began to reign over Israel in the second year of Asa king of Judah, and reigned two years; 1 Kings xv. 25. This was in the twenty-first year of his father, and it contradicts 1 Kings xiv. 20, where we are told that Jeroboam reigned twenty-two years, unless we suppose that father and son reigned jointly.

(7.) Baasha slew Nadab, and began to reign over Israel in the third year of Asa; and he reigned in Tirzah twenty-four years; 1 Kings xv. 33.

(8.) In the thirty-sixth year of Asa, Baasha makes war against him; 2 Chron. xvi. 1. Here the years of Asa are probably counted in continuation of those of his grandfather, as Baasha died in the twenty-sixth year of Asa; 1 Kings xvi. 8.

(9.) Elah, the son of Baasha, began to reign in the twenty-sixth of Asa, and he reigned for two years; 1 Kings xvi. 8.

(10.) In the twenty-seventh of Asa, Zimri slew Elah, and reigned for seven days over Israel; 1 Kings xvi. 15. We have omitted his name from the table. Then Omri and Tibni divided the kingdom of Israel.

Omri reigned twelve years, for the first six in Tirzah, and for the last six in Samaria, the new capital of Israel; 1 Kings, xvi. 23.   Tibni reigned five years, dying in the thirty-first of Asa, leaving Omri to reign for seven years over all Israel; 1 Kings xvi. 22.

(11.) Ahab, the son of Omri, began to reign in the thirty-eighth of Asa, and reigned over Israel in Samaria twenty-two years; 1 Kings xvi. 29.

(12.) Jehoshaphat, the son of Asa, began to reign over Judah in the fourth year of Ahab, and reigned twenty-five years; 1 Kings xxii. 41.

(13.) Ahaziah, the son of Ahab, began to reign over Israel in the seventeenth of Jehoshaphat, and reigned two years; 1 Kings xxii. 51.   This contradicts 1 Kings xvi. 29, by shortening Ahab's reign, unless we suppose that the son reigned jointly with his father, which is very possible, though not allowed by 1 Kings xxii. 40, which says he reigned in his stead.

(14.) Jehoram, the son of Ahab, succeeded his brother in the eighteenth year of Jehoshaphat, and reigned twelve years over Israel; 2 Kings iii. 1. The first two years of his reign were also jointly with his father, unless, as before remarked, we shorten the father's reign.

(15.) In the fifth year of Joram king of Israel, Jehoram, the son of Jehoshaphat, began to reign over Judah while his father was yet alive.   He reigned eight years; 2 Kings viii. 16, 17.   As the father and son are here said to have reigned jointly, as did David and his son Solomon, it is not unreasonable to suppose that it may have been the same with other kings, when the historian has not expressly said so.

(16.) We read in 2 Kings i. 17, that in the second year of Jehoram king of Judah, Jehoram of Israel succeeded to his brother Ahaziah. But this date can in no way be reconciled with what we have learned from other passages. See notes (14) and (15).

(17.) Ahaziah, king of Judah, began to reign in the eleventh year of Joram king of Israel, 2 Kings ix. 29, or in the twelfth year, according to 2 Kings viii. 25. This latter date seems the more probable. He reigned one year. He is called Jehoahaz in 2 Chron. xxi. 17.

(18.) Jehu, who had slain Jehoram king of Israel, reigned twenty-eight years; 2 Kings x. 36.

(19.) Ahaziah, king of Judah, was slain at the same time as Jehoram king of Israel, 2 Kings ix. 27, and he was succeeded by his mother, Athaliah, who reigned seven years; 2 Kings xi. 4. In the verse before we are told that the child, the rightful king, was hidden for only six years. This may be explained by note (4), where we learn that six years may easily get counted for seven regnal years.

(20.) In the seventh year of Jehu, Jehoash began to reign over Judah. He reigned forty years; 2 Kings xii. 1.

(21.) In the twenty-third year of Jehoash, Jehoahaz, the son of Jehu, began to reign over Israel, and reigned seventeen years; 2 Kings xiii. 1.

(22.) In the thirty-seventh year of Jehoash of Judah, Jehoash, the son of Jehoahaz, began to reign over Israel, and reigned sixteen years; 2 Kings xiii. 10.

(23.) In the second year of Jehoash of Israel, Amaziah, the son of Jehoash of Judah, began to reign, and he reigned twenty-nine years; 2 Kings xiv. 1: he survived Jehoash of Israel fifteen years; 2 Kings xiv. 17. Then his son began in the so-called twenty-seventh of Jeroboam; 2 Kings xv. 1.

(24). In the fifteenth year of Amaziah, Jeroboam began to reign over Israel, and reigned forty-one years; 2 Kings xiv. 23. This can only be reconciled with other quotations by supposing that he then began to reign alone, after having reigned thirteen years jointly with his father.—See note (26). Here, then, we shorten the usual chronology.

(25.) Azariah, or Uzziah, son of Amaziah, reigned fifty-two years over Judah; 2 Kings xv. 2. We place his beginning in the sixth year of his father's reign. If we followed the usual chronology, and made him begin in the twenty-seventh of Jeroboam, we should have to place an interregnum of twelve years in Israel between Jeroboam and his son Zachariah, as is done in the margin of the Authorized Version of the Bible.

(26.) In the twenty-seventh year of Jeroboam, says the historian, Azariah began to reign; 2 Kings xv. 1. This was fifteen years after the death of Jehoash of Israel; 2 Kings xiv. 17. Hence it is clear that Jeroboam had reigned twelve years jointly with his father.

(27.) In the thirty-eighth year of Azariah, Zachariah began to reign over Israel. He reigned for six months; 2 Kings xv. 8. He succeeded on the death of Jeroboam his father; 2 Kings xiv. 29; but the usual chronology places an interregnum between them.

(28.) In the thirty-ninth year of the reign of Uzziah, Shallum reigned for one month over Israel; 2 Kings xv. 13.

(29.) Also in the thirty-ninth year of Azariah, or Uzziah, Menahem began to reign over Israel, and he reigned ten years; 2 Kings xv. 17.

(30.) The forty-ninth year of Azariah is unaccounted for in Israel. Perhaps Menahem reigned eleven years.

(31.) In the fiftieth year of Azariah, Pekahiah, the son of Menahem, began to reign over Israel, and reigned two years; 2 Kings xv. 23.

(32.) In the fifty-second year of Azariah, Pekah, having slain Pekahiah, began to reign in Israel. He reigned twenty years; 2 Kings xv. 27.

(33.) In the second year of Pekah, Jotham, the son of Uzziah, began to reign over Judah, and reigned sixteen years; 2 Kings xv. 32.

(34.) In the seventeenth year of Pekah, Ahaz, the son of Jotham, began to reign, and reigned sixteen years; 2 Kings xvi. 1. This must be understood to mean that he then began to reign alone at the death of his father, after having reigned seven years as his colleague. This is confirmed by the quotations in the next note, and makes it unnecessary to place an interregnum between Pekah and Hoshea, who slew him, as is done in the margin of the Authorized Version.

(35.) Hoshea began to reign over Israel in the twelfth year of Ahaz, and reigned nine years; 2 Kings xvii. 1. He slew his predecessor Pekah in the twentieth year of Jotham; 2 Kings xv. 30. The two dates mean the same year ; though Jotham had been dead four years, his years were still used in dating events.

(36.) In the third year of Hoshea, Hezekiah began to reign over Judah, and reigned twenty-nine years; 2 Kings xviii. 1.   But we place the beginning of his reign one year later, agreeably with the two following quotations.

(37.) The fourth year of Hezekiah was the seventh of Hoshea. In that year Shalmanezer, king of Assyria, besieged Samaria ; 2 Kings xviii. 9.

(38.) The sixth year of Hezekiah was the ninth of Hoshea. In that year the monarchy of Israel came to an end ; 2 Kings xvii. 6 ; xviii. 10.

(39.) The year B.C. 721 was the first year of Mardoc Empadus king of Babylon, by an eclipse of the moon observed in Babylon, and recorded by Claudius Ptolemy. He is called Berodach Baladan in the Hebrew; and he sends an embassy to Hezekiah, perhaps about 15 years before the death of the latter, or about B.C. 713 ; 2 Kings xx. 6–12. Mardoc Empadus died B.C. 709.

(40.) Manasseh succeeded his father Hezekiah, and reigned fifty-five years; 2 Kings xxi. 1. Henceforth we have no kings of Israel for the historian to make use of their years in dating the kings of Judah.

(41.) Amon succeeded his father, Manasseh, and reigned two years ; 2 Kings xxi. 19.

(42.) Josiah succeeded his father Amon, and reigned thirty-one years ; 2 Kings xxii. 1.

(43.) Jeremiah begins to prophesy in the thirteenth year of Josiah ; Jerem. xxv. 3.—See note (46).

(44.) The year B.C. 621 was the fifth year of Nabopulassar, king of Babylon, by an eclipse of the moon, recorded by C. Ptolemy.

(45.) Jehoahaz, called also Shallum, succeeded Josiah, and reigned three months, and then Jehoiakim, called also Eliakim, reigned eleven years; 2 Kings xxiii. 31, 36.

(46.) The fourth year of Jehoiakim was the first of Nebuchadnezzar, and the twenty-third from the thirteenth of Josiah; Jerem. xxv. 1. The Captivity in Babylon was to come to an end in seventy years from this time.

(47.) Jehoiachin, called also Jeconiah, reigned three months, and was then carried into captivity in the eighth year of Nebuchadnezzar; 2 Kings xxiv. 8—12. His series of years, we shall see, was continued under the name of "the Captivity." Some writers make the first year of "the Captivity" follow the first year of Jehoiachin; but this is contradicted by other passages.

(48.) Zedekiah, called also Mattaniah, reigned eleven years, while Jehoiachin was a captive in Babylon; 2 Kings xxiv. 18.

(49.) The fifth year of the Captivity is the year 30 of an era not named; Ezek. i. 1, 2. This is obviously of Nabopulassar. Ezekiel seems to have thought that this year B.C. 596 was 390 after Jeroboam's revolt, which he calls the iniquity of Israel; chap. iv. 5. He thus places Jeroboam's revolt in B.C. 986. Our table places it in B.C. 936, and the margin of the authorized Bible places it in B.C. 975.

(50.) The tenth year of Zedekiah is the eighteenth of Nebuchadnezzar; Jerem. xxxii. 1.

(51.) The City of Jerusalem was smitten in the twelfth year of the Captivity, Ezek. xxxiii. 21, and in the nineteenth of Nebuchadnezzar; 2 Kings xxv. 8. This shows that the years of " the Captivity " were counted from the king's accession, not from his being carried captive.

(52.) The twenty-fifth year of the Captivity is the fourteenth of the City smitten; Ezek. xl. 1.

(53.) Evil Merodach began to reign in the thirty-seventh year of the Captivity; 2 Kings xxv. 27.

(54.) Nabonned of Cl. Ptolemy seems to be the same as Belshazzar of the Book of Daniel.

(55.) The Desolation of seventy years, mentioned in Jeremiah xxv. 11, came to an end in the first year of Cyrus; 2 Chron. xxxvi. 21; Ezra i. 1. The Jewish captives in Babylon then returned home under Prince Zerubbabel.

(56.) Xenophon, in his " Cyropædia," makes Cyaxares II. of Media the conqueror of Babylon; and the Book of Daniel says that it was Darius the Mede who overthrew the Babylonian monarchy. By some these two kings are thought to be the same; but by some their very existence is denied; and Cl. Ptolemy makes Cyrus of Persia the immediate successor of the last king of Babylon. But in favour of there having been such a Median conqueror, we may remark that Jerem. li. 11, and Isaiah xiii. 17, which are later additions to those books, both speak of the Medes as the conquerors of Babylon; and in Isaiah xxi. 2, those nations are spoken of as the joint conquerors. Cyrus reigned nine years.

(57.) The year B.C. 523 was the seventh of Cambyses, by an eclipse of the moon recorded by Cl. Ptolemy. Cambyses reigned eight years.

(58.) In the second year of Darius, Jerusalem had been punished seventy years; Zechariah i. 7, 12.

The years of the Babylonian kings, after the overthrow of the Assyrians and before their own overthrow, are in Cl. Ptolemy fewer by one than in our table; thus—

	As above.	In Cl. Ptolemy.
Nabopulassar . .	18 years.	20 years.
Nebuchadnezzar .	43 ,,	43 ,,
Evil Merodach . .	4 ,,	2 ,,
Neriglissor . .	5 ,,	4 ,,
Nabonned . . .	17 ,,	17 ,,
	87	86

(59.) The building of the second Temple was finished in the sixth year of Darius (Ezra vi. 15) by Prince Zerubbabel; Zechariah iv. 9.

(60.) Esther is made queen in Susa, the capital of Persia, by Ahasuerus, who reigned over one hundred and twenty-seven provinces, from India to Ethiopia; Esther i. This was in the third year of his reign. He was probably Xerxes I. Her influence may have obtained for Ezra permission to return to Jerusalem.

(61.) In the seventh year of Artaxerxes, Ezra returns to Jerusalem as the Persian governor of the city; Ezra vii. 8. This was probably in the reign of Xerxes I., called Ahasuerus in the Book of Esther. This was fifty-nine years after the Decree of Cyrus which allowed the first return of the Jews. See Daniel ix. 25, where forty-nine years only are allowed to what seems to be meant for this space of time.

(62.) In the twentieth year, probably of Artaxerxes Longimanus, Nehemiah returns to Jerusalem; Nehemiah i.

ON THE SEVENTY WEEKS OF DANIEL, CHAP. IX.

THE Hebrew word here translated a Week, simply
means a Seven, and is open to the same ambiguity
as the word for Month, which means, a Renewing,
and the word for Year, which means, a Change.   To
clear up the ambiguity, a writer sometimes says, a
"year of days," a "month of days," a "week of
days."   But the context usually makes his meaning
clear, and these fuller expressions are not often used.
Yet their being occasionally used shows the ambiguity which hangs upon the words.   Hence our
commentators take no liberty whatever in understanding the week in this chapter to mean a week
of years, and the seventy weeks spoken of to mean
490 years.   After this preface, we may turn to the
passage in Daniel, of course correcting the authorized version :—

"Know therefore and understand, that from the
going forth of the command (B.C. 538) to lead back
home, and to build up Jerusalem, unto an Anointed
Ruler shall be seven weeks (or forty-nine years ; B.C.
489).   Then in sixty and two weeks (or 434 years)
the Broad Place shall be built again (B.C. 55) and
the ditch, even amid the distress of the times. After
the sixty and two weeks shall an Anointed One be
cut off, and nothing shall remain to him.   And the
people of the Ruler that shall come will destroy the
city and the Holy Place ; and the end thereof will

be with a flood; and until the end of the war, deso-
lations are determined. And he will confirm a treaty
with Many for one week (or seven years). And in
the middle of the week (B.C. 51) he will cause the
sacrifice and the meal offering to cease, and upon the
battlements shall be the abominations of desolation,
even until the consummation, and that which has been
determined, shall be poured out on the desolator."

In the year B.C. 538, the Medes, who may have
been under the command of a sovereign named
Cyaxares II., or Darius, and the Persians, under the
command of Cyrus, conquered Babylon. That both
nations were engaged in the conquest appears from
Isaiah xxi. 2, though the Medes only are mentioned
in Isaiah xiii. 17, and Jeremiah li. 11. The date we
learn from C. Ptolemy, who says that Cyrus reigned
over Babylon nine years, and was then succeeded by
Cambyses. The seventh of Cambyses was B.C. 523,
as fixed by an eclipse of the moon; hence the first
of Cyrus was B.C. 538. In that year the Jewish
captives in Babylon were allowed to return home
and rebuild their Temple. See 2 Chron. xxxvi. 22,
Ezra i. 1. Prince Zerubbabel, or Sheshbazzar, was
the leader who brought them back to their own
country.

That year B.C. 538 is also fixed for the return
of the captives, by a passage added by some writer
who lived at that time, to the writings of Jeremiah.
Jerem. xxv. 1—14, tells us that for seventy years
after Nebuchadnezzar's accession, or after the fourth
year of Jehoiakim, the land shall be desolate, and
in subjection to the king of Babylon. See page
25, where the fourth of Jehoiakim is shown to be

B.C. 607; and thus the seventieth year from that time is B.C. 538.

The year B.C. 479 may be certainly shown to be the seventh year of Xerxes I. It is the twelfth year after the eclipse of the moon B.C. 491, in the thirty-first of Darius; and Darius reigned, according to C. Ptolemy, thirty-six years. It was in that year that Ezra, the Jewish high priest, was made ruler of Jerusalem by the Persian king, Artaxerxes. See Ezra vii. 7. The Persian kings' names are used by various historians rather indiscriminately; the Xerxes I. of the Greek writers is probably the Arta-xerxes of Ezra, and the Ahasuerus of Esther i. 1. That year is fifty-nine years—not forty-nine years—after the command to build up the Temple. Here, then, if Ezra is the Anointed Ruler of Dan. ix. 25, our chronology seems at fault. The year B.C. 55 is, however, 49 years and 434 years later than B.C. 538, and in this year we ought to have, not the Temple, but its fortifications rebuilt, if we are right in believing that the year B.C. 538 is the point from which Daniel's seventy weeks are to be counted. The writer who added this chapter to the book of Daniel may have been mistaken in Ezra's date, but he is less likely to have been uncertain as to how long an event in his own day was from the first year of Cyrus's reign.

Josephus, in his "History of the Jews," writes with so little chronological method, that it is not easy to fix with exactness the date of the events mentioned. But it was about B.C. 55 that Hyrcanus began to rebuild the walls of Jerusalem in sadly troublous times, to defend himself against Alexander, the son of his brother Aristobulus, with whom he had been carrying on a civil war. The two brothers each claimed the throne of Judea ; but Aristobulus had been carried prisoner to Rome, and Alexander was continuing the war for him. See Antiq. xiv. v. 2, and Wars, 1, viii. 2. Gabinius, however, the Roman general, after a time, overruns the whole country. After besieging several cities, he takes Hyrcanus prisoner ; he brings him to Jerusalem, where he allows him the care of the Temple ; but he declares the monarchy to be at an end, and he arranges that the political government of the country shall be carried on for the future by an Aristocracy, classed in five councils established in five different cities. See Wars, 1, viii. 5, and Antiq. xiv. v. 4. This form of government continued for the next eleven years; and before it came to an end, Aristobulus and his son Alexander had both been put to death. We may be quite sure that when Gabinius was master of Jerusalem, he placed upon the walls of the city the Roman standards, those ensigns of conquest, which were made yet more hateful to the Jews because they were objects of idolatrous worship to the Roman soldiers.

Here, then, we have all the circumstances mentioned by Daniel. The Broad Place, or Temple Area, and the ditch which guards it on the east and south sides are repaired amid the distress of the times. The Anointed One, King Aristobulus, is cut off, as also is his son. The Romans conquer the country, and make a treaty with Many, or the Aristocracy, in place of a monarch. The Roman standards, the Abominations of Desolation, are placed on the battlements, and we have no difficulty in believing that the

daily sacrifice and meal offering ceased.   The only
flaw in our reasoning seems to be, that we know of
no Anointed Ruler forty-nine years after the return
from captivity.   Ezra, who most nearly suits the
requirements of the case, was made Ruler fifty-nine
years after the return.

The author of this chapter in the book of Daniel
would seem to have written it in the year B.C. 51,
that is, half a week, or three years, before his
seventy weeks were to come to an end.

THE CHRONOLOGY OF CHRIST'S MINISTRY.

THIS is a subject which will by most persons be
granted to be of some importance.   If we could
determine with reasonable certainty the time of the
baptism and that of the crucifixion, we should know
the length of the ministry ; and this would help us
materially to a right understanding of the life, and
thence of the teachings of Jesus.   Again, if we
knew the year of the crucifixion, we should know, by
the help of the Jewish law and customs, the day of
the week on which the Passover supper was eaten,
and thence whether Jesus ate that supper with his
disciples, as we are told in the first three Gospels,
or whether he was put to death before the Passover,
as we are told in the fourth Gospel.   At present,
opinions are so much divided on these matters, that
the subject has seemed to be in hopeless confusion,

But I venture to think that, with a more patient and thorough inquiry, the doubts might yet be removed.

The reason why these difficulties have not been cleared up, seems to arise from the less common books which must be read, and from the less agreeable line of study which must be followed, for that purpose. Our scholars are too much confined to the classical writers of antiquity, who can in this case give them no help. A date cannot be understood with exactness unless we understand the almanac or mode of dating in use at the time and in the country to which it relates; and many of our scholars who have given an opinion about the chronology of the New Testament, may perhaps never have looked at the Mishna, in Treatise Rosh Hashanah, or at Censorinus "De die Natali," or at C. Ptolemy's Astronomical work, or at Theon's and Heraclius's fragments on the ancient year, or have examined a series of Egyptian and Asiatic coins of the Roman emperors, or even have looked to the method of dating employed in the Hebrew Books of Kings. Yet most, or rather all, of these authorities have to be studied in order to understand the time meant by those very simple words of Luke's Gospel, "the fifteenth year of Tiberius Cæsar;" although it is perfectly well known that Tiberius became emperor on the death of Augustus on the 19th August, A.D. 14. To this point I shall first confine myself.

ON THE YEAR OF THE BAPTISM.

WE read in Luke's Gospel (iii. 1) that Jesus was baptized by John in the 15th year of Tiberius. Our

inquiry, therefore, is on what days did that year
begin and end, according to the mind of the writer?
But we shall make the question more simple if we
state it thus : the first year of Tiberius began on the
19th of August, A.D. 14 ; when did his second year
begin? And I propose to show that the first year,
according to the mode of civil reckoning in use at
the time, contained only ten days ; that the New-
year's day was the 29th of August; and that, therefore, on the 29th of August, A.D. 14, begin the
second year of Tiberius ; and accordingly that the
fifteenth year began on the 29th of August, A.D. 27.

Perhaps no English work on ancient chronology
stands higher, or deserves to stand higher, than
Clinton's Fasti. He begins his Fasti Romani with
these words, which contain the error which I wish to
refute : " The death of Augustus, Aug. 19, A.D. 14,
was in the fifth month before these tables [his Fasti
Romani] commence, which begin Kal. Jan., A.D. 15,
and *contain the last 7 m. 19 d. of the first year
of Tiberius.*" This last statement of Clinton an
hardly be called untrue, because it would be tru if
stated of Queen Victoria instead of Tiberius ; bu I
propose to show that it is untrue to the extent of
355 days, if made use of when reading a date in
any ancient writer who dates by means of a regnal
year ; and that Clinton should have said that his
Tables would contain the last 7 m. 29 d. of the
second year of Tiberius. Clinton's mistake is made
in the assumption that an ancient regnal year began
and ended with the accession day, which it does with
the kings of modern Europe. But, against this, it
may be shown that the regnal year with the ancient

writers always began and ended with the civil New-year's day, excepting, of course, the first and last years of a reign, each of which contained only some odd months or days. With us the last year of a reign contains only some odd months or days; with the ancients, the first year also was equally incomplete. The last year of one king or emperor, and the first year of his successor together contained twelve months.

To establish this point, let us read first in the First Book of Kings. We there find (xv. 25) that Nadab, king of Israel, began to reign in the second year of Asa king of Judah, and reigned two years; and yet Baasha (xv. 33) began in the third year of Asa. Again, Baasha, beginning in the third year of Asa, reigned 24 years, and yet Elah, his son, began in the 26th year of Asa, 1 Kings xvi. 8. Again, Elah, beginning in the 26th year of Asa, reigned two years, and yet Zimri killed him in the 27th year of Asa, 1 Kings xvi. 10. It is unnecessary to multiply instances from the Hebrew writers. The two years of Elah's reign mean parts of two years. Deeds, perhaps, had been dated in his first and second year. A New-year's day had happened between his accession and his death; and these quotations prove that in each of these cases the first year, like the last year, contained only some odd months or days.

Moreover, this is not a mere inference from the apparent contradiction in the above quotations from the Book of Kings; but the Jewish work, the Mishna, written about A.D. 150, in the Treatise Rosh Hashanah, *on the New-year's day,* begins by saying that regnal years were reckoned from the New-year's day; that is, not from the accession-day, as with us. The Mishna, however, says that of the four days on which, for various purposes, the year was said to begin, the regnal year began on 1st Nisan, which we shall have to show was not the legal New-year's day used by Eastern subjects of the Roman emperor.

The Alexandrian coins of the Roman emperors, which are usually dated with a regnal year, quite confirm this mode of reckoning. Thus Galba reigned seven months, but we have Alexandrian coins dated in the first and second year of his reign, because the New-year's day fell within that space of time. So Titus died in September after a reign of only two years and three months; but as that space of time contained three New-years' days, we have coins dated in his fourth year. The Alexandrian coins of the last year of Nero, of Domitian, of Trajan, of Hadrian, and others, in each case claiming for them a year more than the historian allows, might in the same way be quoted to prove that the first year of an emperor's reign contained only the few months or days which passed between his accession-day and the next New-year's day. Elagabalus reigned three years and nine months, and yet, as Gibbon mentions with surprise, we have coins dated in his 5th year.

This mode of reckoning was also used under the Greek kings, the Ptolemies, as may be proved from Porphyry's chronology of their reigns, printed in Scaliger's Eusebius. Thus Porphyry says that Philadelphus reigned 38 years; and the well-established chronology of those kings confirms this; but we have a coin dated in the 39th year of his reign.

We now proceed to determine upon what day of the natural year, or rather of our year, the civil New-year's day fell for those parts of the Roman empire which dated by means of regnal years. But we must first remind the reader that in Rome, and in the West, wherever the Latin language was used, the regnal year was unknown. The Romans dated by consulships, which began in January and ended in December, unless any political event cut a consulship short in the middle. The Latin writers do not speak of an emperor's reign, or count his years by any expression, except his consulships or Tribunician power; to do so would be to consider him as a king, while he never assumed any title but those which were used under the republic. But it was otherwise in the East. In Egypt, Syria, Babylonia, and Asia Minor, the people had been used to kings; and in a very few years after Octavianus, afterwards called Augustus, had made himself sole master of Rome and its provinces, all these provinces dated by the years of his reign, as they had before dated by their own Greek kings, the successors of Alexander, using the same calendar and New-year's day that they had before used. This we now proceed to show was the 29th of August.

Claudius Ptolemy has preserved a series of Babylonian and Alexandrian eclipses and occultations of the moon, recorded sometimes by means of the regnal year of the kings of Babylon, as Nabopulassar and his Persian successors Cambyses and Darius,

and sometimes by the regnal year of the Alexandrian
kings, as Philadelphus, Philometor, and their
Roman successors Domitian and Hadrian. In all
these cases modern astronomical science has proved
that the year used consisted of 365 days only,
without an intercalary day or leap-year. Hence the
New-year's day in these countries was always moving
at the rate of one day in four years. Censorinus,
who wrote on the various eras in use, tells us that
in his day, in the consulship of Ulpius and Pontia-
nus, 991 of Rome, 562 of Alexander's death [that is,
in A.D. 238], this movable New-year's day was vii.
Kal. Jul. [or 25th June], but that 100 years earlier
it had been xii. Kal. Aug. [or 21st July]. This in-
formation is fully confirmed by all the above-mentioned astronomical observations, which in Halma's
edition of C. Ptolemy have been carefully calculated
and made to throw all the required light upon chronology. Following up this knowledge, we easily
learn that in the year B.C. 25, which the Egyptians
called the 5th year of Augustus, the movable New-
year's day was the 29th of August. There it was
fixed for the future for all those countries which had
previously used the movable New-year's day, because
at that time the Julian year was introduced into
Alexandria by the emperor. This we are told by
the astronomer Theon, in an extract published by
Cory in his Ancient Fragments. He there says
that at Midsummer, in the 100th year of Diocletian, there had been 102 intercalary days, or leap-
years, in Alexandria; that is, that the leap-year of
B.C. 21 was the first leap-year in Alexandria. On
that year, as we have said, the New-year's day was

the 29th August, and there it was fixed for the
future by the introduction of leap-years. And more
exactly Heraclius, in a fragment " On how to find
the Day of the Week in each Month, and which
Years are Leap-Years," published by Dodwell, with
his Dissertationes Cyprianicæ, says, "The day which
we call the 29th of August, the Alexandrians call
the 1st of Thoth," their New-year's day. And this
is again enlarged upon by Theon in a fragment on
the Calendar, also published by Dodwell in the same
volume, where he says that from the fifth year of
the reign of Augustus the Egyptians introduced the
Julian method of adding a quarter of a day to the
length of the year.

The provinces of Babylonia, Syria, Asia Minor,
and Egypt, all made use of this civil year which we
have been describing ; only so far varying, that while
some cities counted by the year of the emperor's
reign, others counted from the era of the Seleucidæ,
and others from the era of Antioch. That the Greeks
of the province of Syria made use of the same, or
nearly the same, New-year's day, may be shown by
their coins, of which we have many dated by those
eras, and bearing the emperor's name, and which
were struck, some in the first and some in the last
year of the reign. Had the New-year's day been
much removed from the end of August, the years by
which those coins are dated would in some cases
have fallen beyond the emperor's reign. Indeed,
no other mode of dating was known in the Roman
world in that century ; but either by the year of
the consulship, which began in January, or by the
Greek year of the Olympiads, which began at Mid-

summer, or by the Greco-Asiatic or Greco-Egyptian year, which began on 29th August, or by the old Egyptian year, which for want of a leap-year began when Luke was writing on 16th August, and was used by none but the astronomers and astrologers. These two last were the only modes by which a regnal year was ever counted before the reign of Diocletian.

ON THE YEAR OF THE CRUCIFIXION.

HAVING thus shown reason for believing that the evangelist Luke meant, by the fifteenth year of Tiberius, a year beginning on 29th August, A.D. 27, it will be unnecessary to show that Clement of Alexandria, when speaking of the crucifixion as happening in the sixteenth year of Tiberius, meant a year beginning on 29th August, A.D. 28, and that as the day of the crucifixion was near the spring equinox, he considered it to have happened in A.D. 29. His words are as follows : " When fixing the time of the Passion more exactly in the sixteenth year of Tiberius Cæsar, some say that the Saviour suffered on the 25th of the month Phamenoth, some on the 25th of Pharmuthi, and some on the 19th of Pharmuthi." (Strom. I. p. 147.) Thus there were three traditions about the exact day of the crucifixion in A.D. 29, namely, Monday, 21st March, Thursday, 14th April, and Wednesday, 20th April. All were agreed upon the year ; they only differed about the day of the month and day of the week.

Tertullian, who wrote about the same time with

Clement, namely, about A.D. 210, agrees with him in the year of the crucifixion, though not in the day, saying, "Which suffering by Him of dismissal [that is crucifixion] was completed under Tiberius Cæsar in the consulship of Rubellius Geminus and Rufius Geminus, in the month of March at the time of the Passover, on the seventh day of the Calends of April, on the first day of unleavened bread, on which they slew the lamb, as had been commanded by Moses." (Adv. Judæos liber, cap. viii.) It is unnecessary to bring proof of what nobody disputes, namely, that the two Gemini were consuls from January to July in A.D. 29. The day fixed upon by Tertullian, therefore, is Saturday, 26th March, which he at the same time declares to have been the day of the Passover.

Origen, who wrote about thirty years later than Clement and Tertullian, in his work against Celsus, agrees with this year so far as to say that the Temple at Jerusalem was destroyed forty-two years after the crucifixion. This may be understood as agreeing with our view of there being about forty-one years and a half between the spring of A.D. 29 and the autumn of A.D. 70, when the Temple was destroyed by Titus; and it will not allow us to place the crucifixion in any later year than A.D. 29.

All later writers must be supposed to be guided by these, unless the contrary can be shown. Thus Lactantius gives us the same day of the year in the consulship of the two Gemini as Tertullian; but he contradicts himself when he adds that it was in the fifteenth of Tiberius, which we have shown, in the mouth of a Greek or Asiatic, would have meant A.D. 28; unless we suppose that in the mouth of a Latin

writer it may possibly have meant A.D. 29. So Julius
Africanus, as quoted by Eusebius in his Chronicle,
places the crucifixion in the sixteenth year of Tiberius;
but then, like Lactantius, he contradicts himself by
adding that was in the second year of the 202nd
Olympiad, which would make it two years later.

It is unnecessary to add more quotations, which
would all be of little value compared with these.
Resting, therefore, upon Clement and Tertullian,
supported as they are by Origen and Lactantius, we
may take it as proved that the crucifixion took place
in A.D. 29, unless doubt can be thrown upon this by
any writers of equal value. But it may be as well
to repeat that the reason why the date of the crucifixion has hitherto been thought doubtful, is because
the mode of counting the regnal years used by the
Greeks in the East has not been understood; and
hence Tertullian's date has been thought to be
contradicted by Clement, and both of these by the
evangelist Luke. Thus Dr. Strauss places the
baptism in A.D. 29, while we have shown it may have
been as early as September, A.D. 27; and others
place the crucifixion in A.D. 30, while we have shown
that the early authorities all agree in A.D. 29.

We thus have arrived at the conclusion that the
ministry of Jesus did not exceed nineteen months,
that it began after the 29th of August A.D. 27, and
ended at the Passover of A.D. 29.

ON THE DAY OF THE PASSOVER IN A.D. 29.

I AM indebted to Professor Adams for the infor-
mation that in A.D. 29, the first new moon after the

spring equinox took place at Jerusalem on Saturday, the 2nd April, at 8 P.M. I have since had this confirmed by the Astronomer-Royal, in a paper signed by Mr. Hind. Hence, according to the usual understanding of the Mosaic Law, Sunday, April 3rd, was the first day of the month Nisan, and the Passover supper was eaten by twilight in the evening of Saturday, April 16th, which was the fourteenth of Nisan. See Exodus xii.; Leviticus xxiii.; Numbers ix.

To this whole train of reasoning, by which it is argued that the Passover supper in the year of the crucifixion was eaten on a Saturday, I know of no objection that can be made, unless it be argued that the month of Nisan took place a lunation earlier, following the new moon of March 3rd; and that Friday, March 4th, was the first of Nisan; and that therefore the 14th of Nisan when the Passover was eaten was Thursday, the 17th of March. But this is opposed to the opinion of the modern Jews, who, guided as they profess to be in the arrangement of their calendar by Maimonides, fix the Passover at the full moon which follows the spring equinox.

In this the Jews are supported by Christian testimony. When the Council of Nicæa, in A.D. 325, decreed that the Christians should keep their feast, not with the Jews at the full moon, but on the first Sunday which followed the full moon, they made no change in the lunation by which the feast was fixed. And Epiphanius says that when God through this Council guided the Church in respect to the feast of Easter, they settled that it took place when the fourteenth day of the moon fell after the spring

E

equinox (Adv. Hæres. III. i. xii.). He had before
said that the natural year as arranged by God does
not end before the equinox (Adv. Hæres. III. i. xi.).
The Mosaic law is not so explicit; but it goes to
confirm this view. The month or lunation that we
have been speaking of is there named Abib, as being
the month when barley is in ear and becomes ripe in
Judea. The day after the Passover supper was the
feast of unleavened bread (see Leviticus xxiii.); and on
the morrow after the Sabbath (or feast of unleavened
bread), that is the sixteenth day of the month Abib,
a sheaf of ripe barley was to be brought to the priest.
Now our travellers tell us that even in the warmest
parts of Judea the barley is not ripe before the 1st
of April; thus confirming our view, founded both
on Jewish and Christian tradition, that the Passover
supper was far less likely to have been eaten in that
year so early as Thursday, 17th March, than one
month later, on Saturday, 16th April.

ON THE DAY OF THE CRUCIFIXION.

§ 1st in Matthew, Mark, and Luke.

WE have already quoted Tertullian as saying that
Jesus was crucified on Saturday, the 26th of March;
and Clement as mentioning three days as spoken of
for that event, Monday, the 21st of March, Thursday, the 14th of April, and Wednesday, the 20th of
April. Now, if we compare these four days, first
with the two possible days mentioned above for the
Passover feast, and, secondly, with the statement

in which all the Gospels agree, namely, that the crucifixion took place in the latter half of the week, we shall see that the only result we can arrive at is, that he was crucified two days before the Passover, that the day was Thursday, the 14th of April, and that the Passover was eaten on Saturday, the 16th of April. And we thus arrive at the conclusion that the external evidence, independent of the New Testament writers, goes to confirm the fourth Gospel, rather than the first three Gospels, in the history of the Last Supper and the Crucifixion.

This opinion that the crucifixion took place on a Thursday is, however, opposed to the uniform belief of the last fifteen centuries, which seems to have been founded upon the belief that the word "Preparation" (Matt. xxvii. 62; Mark xv. 42; Luke xxiii. 54) was used for Friday. But we may remark that it is not opposed to the opinion of Clement and Tertullian, who neither of them seem to fix upon a Friday. And even if our determination of the days of the week from their days of the month be doubted, yet, in the case of Clement, it is clear that he had no belief that the day of the week was certainly Friday, because of the three days that he mentions, no two can be on the same day of the week. Let us see how far our opinion is supported by the Gospels. If Jesus was crucified at noon on Friday, and buried after sunset on that evening, and the tomb was found empty on Sunday morning, the body was less than thirty-six hours in the tomb, which very little agrees with the expected time, so often mentioned in the Gospels. Matthew (xii. 40) says that the Son of Man is to be "three days and three nights in the heart of the earth," and in three other places (xvi. 21, xvii. 23, xx. 19) says that he is expected to rise from the dead " on the third day." Mark also in two places (ix. 31, x. 34), and Luke in three (ix. 22, xviii. 33, xxiv. 7, 46), repeat that he is expected to rise "on the third day." Indeed, in both places in Mark, and in two in Luke, some of the oldest MSS. have " after three days." Now the evangelists certainly mean us to understand that these expectations were fulfilled; and hence we can hardly suppose that they meant to say that the body was in the tomb for a shorter period than three nights and two days, namely from Thursday evening till Sunday morning.

If we now turn to the narrative in the Gospels, we shall find that our fixing upon Thursday or Friday for the crucifixion will depend upon whether we understand that some of the actions there described took place on the Sabbath or no. Luke alone says (xxiii. 56), "they rested on the Sabbath." But if we are allowed to carry this remark into the other Gospels, and to suppose that neither high-priests nor disciples did anything on the Sabbath, we shall then find that Matthew most clearly, and Mark with less certainty, place the crucifixion on Thursday, while Luke, omitting some of the events, places it on Friday. Of the fourth we must speak separately. Treating the Sabbath as a day without events, the narrative in Matthew is as follows:

Ch. xxvi. 17. On the first day of unleavened bread the disciples prepare the Passover, and eat it with Jesus in the evening. That night Jesus is betrayed to the priests. This I call Wednesday.

Ch. xxvii. 1. On the next morning he is taken before Pilate; he is crucified at the sixth hour, or noon; he dies at the ninth hour, or three o'clock. In the evening Joseph obtains the body from Pilate, and buries it. This I call Thursday; and we shall see that it is the evening of the preparation.

Ch. xxvii. 62. On the morrow, which is after the preparation, the high-priests and Pharisees come to Pilate and obtain a guard of soldiers, and themselves seal the tomb. This I call Friday; it cannot be Saturday, because of the rest upon the Sabbath. On Friday evening at sunset the Sabbath begins, and nothing is done till sunset on Saturday.

Ch. xxviii. 1. On the morning of Sunday, the first day of the week, the two Maries come to the tomb and find it empty.

The agreement and disagreement of Mark and Luke with the above will be shown most conveniently in the following table, remembering that in each Gospel the days must be counted backwards from the first day of the week, which is the only day certainly mentioned in any of the narratives.

	MATTHEW.	MARK.	LUKE.
Wednesday.	xxvi. 17. First day of unleavened bread. The disciples prepare the Passover. xxvi. 20. In the evening the Supper is eaten ; Jesus is betrayed.	xiv. 12. First day of unleavened bread. The disciples prepare the Passover. xiv. 17. In the evening the Supper is eaten ; Jesus is betrayed.	
Thursday.	xxvii. 1. In the morning he is led to Pilate, and crucified at noon. xxvii. 57. In the evening Joseph begs for the body, buries it, and rolls a stone on the door of the tomb. [It is the Preparation.]	xv. 1. In the morning he is led to Pilate, and crucified at noon. xv. 42. In the evening, it is the Preparation, a Prosabbaton, Joseph begs for the body, buys a cloth, buries Jesus, rolls a stone on the door of the tomb.	xxii. 7. The da of unleavened bread The disciples prepar the Passover. xxii. 14. When th hour is come the Sup per is eaten ; Jesus i betrayed.
Friday.	xxvii. 62. On the morrow after the Preparation the high-priests get a guard from Pilate and seal the tomb. [In the evening the Sabbath begins.]	 [In the evening the Sabbath begins.]	xxii. 66. When i was day he is led t Pilate, and crucifie at noon. xxiii. 52. Josep begs for the body, an buries it. That da is the Preparation ; Sabbath is dawning The women prepar spices and ointments
Saturday.	[The Sabbath, when nothing is done.]	[The Sabbath, when nothing is done.] xvi. 1. When the Sabbath is passed the disciples buy spices.	xxiii. 56. The rested on the Sabbatl according to the com mandment.
Sunday.	xxviii. 1. At dawn of the first day of the week the two Maries come to the tomb.	xvi. 2. Early on the first day of the week they come to the tomb.	xxiv. 1. By day break on the first da of the week the dis ciples come to th tomb.

Here it will be observed, that if the crucifixion took place on Friday, according to the common opinion, Matthew would describe the priests as violating the Sabbath by taking a guard and sealing the tomb on the next morning; Mark would make Joseph violate the Sabbath by buying a cloth and burying Jesus on Friday after sunset, though the same Gospel describes the disciples as respecting the Sabbath by not buying their spices till after sunset on Saturday. Luke seems not to have been aware that the Sabbath began at sunset on Friday. He alone clearly describes the disciples as violating the Sabbath. He says that on the night of the crucifixion, when the Sabbath was dawning, Joseph buries the body, and the women prepare spices and ointments; and yet he then adds, " they rested on the Sabbath, according to the commandment." He seems not to have been aware that the Sabbath had already begun with sunset on Friday, and that he was describing a breach of the Sabbath. Thus of the first three Gospels, Luke alone, while showing a want of familiarity with Jewish customs, places the crucifixion on Friday; the other two will both appear more consistent if we suppose them to place that event on Thursday, and simply to have omitted from their narrative the remark, to a Jewish reader so very unnecessary, that nothing was done on the Sabbath, and hence that none of the events mentioned took place on that day.

The Mishna, in the Treatise Sabbath, would leave us rather in doubt about the act of Joseph in laying Jesus in the tomb on the Sabbath-day, because though it forbids the carrying a corpse to burial on that day (ch. x. 5), yet it allows the anointing and washing it and doing what is barely needful (ch. xxiii. 5): here in the case of a person crucified Joseph would seem to have been allowed to lay it in the tomb, which was close at hand; but the sealing the tomb by the high-priest, mentioned in Matt. xxvii. 66, the buying a cloth, and rolling the stone to the door of the tomb by Joseph, mentioned in Mark xv. 46, the preparing spices and ointments by the women, mentioned in Luke xxiii. 56, are all acts which we must suppose ought to have been done before the commencement of the Sabbath or before the sunset of Friday; and therefore if they were done in the evening, as the narrative leads us to understand, they must have been done either in breach of the Sabbath or on the evening of Thursday.

§ *2ndly. On the day of the crucifixion in John's Gospel; and on the Preparation.*

Of the fourth Gospel we must speak separately; it has its own difficulties in this portion of the narrative. But before doing so we must consider the meaning of the Preparation, which is mentioned in every Gospel as one of the circumstances by which the day of the crucifixion was dated; but in the fourth Gospel is described as the preparation for the Passover, while in the others it must be understood as a preparation for the Sabbath.

The Mishna, in the Treatise Pesachim, says, that " on the evening previous to the 14th of Nisan it is necessary to make search for leaven by the light of a candle;" and " if no search has been made on the evening preceding the 14th, it must be done on that day;" and quotes one Rabbi who says that in that case it must be done early in the morning of the 14th. This ceremony seems to be the preparation meant. It afterwards adds, that "when the 14th of Nisan happens on the Sabbath, all the leaven must be removed before the Sabbath commences." Thus we learn that when the Passover is eaten on a Saturday evening, this ceremonial search for leaven, which may very reasonably be called a preparation for the Passover, must be begun on Thursday after sunset, and if not finished then must be finished early on the Friday. In the Syriac Gospels the preparation is named the Gehrevah, meaning the *evening* ceremony, because it was to be performed in the dark by candlelight; it was only in case of omission performed on the following morning.

The fourth Gospel says (xviii. 28), that on the morning of the crucifixion the Jews lead Jesus to the Prætorium of the Roman Governor, but go not in themselves, that they might not be defiled, but that they might eat the Passover.

This fear of defilement does not help our inquiry, because such defilement would last a week. We read in Numbers xix. 11, that he that toucheth a dead body shall be unclean for seven days; and in the Mishna, Treatise Pesachim, ch. viii. 8, on the various defilements which will disqualify a man from eating the Passover, that he who has just parted from the uncircumcised must be considered as one who has just parted from a grave.

(Ch. xix. 14.) Pilate gives up Jesus, apparently to the Jews, to be crucified, " and it was the preparation for the Passover, about the sixth hour," or noon.

(Ch. xix. 31.) When Jesus was dead, " the Jews, that the bodies might not remain upon the cross on the Sabbath, because it was the Preparation, for the day of that Sabbath was an high day," asked to have the bodies removed.

(Ch. xix. 42.) Joseph and Nicodemus bury Jesus, in a tomb already made, as it would seem hurriedly, "because of the Jews' Preparation." It is necessary here to depart from the Authorized Version, particularly when it speaks of " the Preparation day," since in the Greek it is simply " the Preparation," and the Syriac Version, as already quoted, makes it rather " the Preparation night."

Now in all this there is nothing to determine the exact day of the crucifixion, except the mention of the Preparation. Our previous reasoning has gone to prove that the Passover was eaten on Saturday evening, and it is confirmed in this case by the custom of the modern Jews, who declare that it must never be eaten on Friday evening, which is the beginning of the Sabbath (See E. H. Lindo's Jewish Calendar). The Preparation was made, or at least begun, on Thursday evening: hence when we are told that the day of the crucifixion was the Preparation, it might be either Thursday or Friday : it might mean it was the day in which the Preparation ought to be made, or that it was the day in which it was completed if omitted on the previous night. But when Jesus is buried, which would seem to have been after sunset, and we are still told that it was the Preparation, and the writer does not say that the Sabbath had begun, the remark would seem to fix the day as Thursday, because by sunset on Friday

the Preparation was over, and the Sabbath had begun. Opinions may differ about the day meant, but
the fourth Gospel cannot be quoted as contradicting
that tradition which places the crucifixion on Thursday, the 14th of April.

The determination of the day of the week on
which the crucifixion took place is, however, of less
importance; our aim has only been to show that it
took place before the Passover supper was eaten, and
that in this respect the fourth Gospel is in all pro-
bability more correct than the first three, which say
that he ate the Passover supper with his disciples
before he was crucified. In this matter the fourth
Gospel is also confirmed by two of the earliest and
least questioned portions of the New Testament:
first, the apostle Paul, in 1 Cor. v. 7, calls Jesus
the Passover slain for us; and, secondly, the book
of Revelation, written probably by the apostle John,
in chap. v. 6, compares him to a Lamb slain. Both
writers must be understood to mean that his death
took place shortly before the Passover supper. The
fixing the day of the week is chiefly interesting in
so far as it agrees with the train of reasoning by
which we fix the year. The astronomical argument,
founded upon our supposing A.D. 29 to be the year
of the crucifixion, gives us Saturday, the 16th of
April, for the Passover; and of the three traditions
recorded by Clement, that which best agrees with
this gives us Thursday, the 14th of April, for the
crucifixion; and then it is satisfactory to find that
the weight of evidence furnished by the Gospels
leans also to a Thursday.

The strongest objection to our train of reasoning

is, that the preparation, παρασκευη, is the distinct
name of Friday evening in Josephus and in some of
the early Christian writers, as being the preparation
for the Sabbath; and hence it came to mean the
whole day Friday. But it will be observed that of
the four Gospels John certainly does not so use the
word; he speaks of the preparation for the Passover,
not the preparation for the Sabbath. Clement and
Tertullian do not so understand it, as they do not
propose Friday for the crucifixion. Moreover, it
seems improbable that Matthew should be so using
it. He speaks of " the morrow, which is after the
preparation." Now if that had been the morning of
the Sabbath, he would certainly have said so, and
not have used such an indirect mode of describing
it. Mark, indeed, does explain the preparation as
a προσαββατον, or *evening before a Sabbath.* But
that does not prove that he means Friday evening,
because other solemn days besides Saturday were
sometimes called Sabbaths. Thus in Leviticus xvi.
31 and xxiii. 32, the fast day on the tenth of the
seventh month is called a Sabbath; and the Sabbath
spoken of in Leviticus xxiii. 11, 16, is understood
to mean the sixteenth of Nisan, the great day of
the Feast of Unleavened Bread. And again, the
" second-first Sabbath" spoken of in Luke vi. 1,
must be understood to mean, not a Saturday, but
a new-moon day in one of those months to which
the Jewish calendar allows two new-moon days.
Luke alone declares the Preparation to be Friday
evening by saying that a Sabbath was dawning.

It is not necessary to say much about the objection
that the preparation for the Passover was killing the

lamb for the supper, which took place on the same day, a few hours before sunset, because that is contradicted by Mark and Luke, who place it in the evening after the sunset, and by the Syriac version of the Gospels, which by the word Gehrevah shows that it took place in the dark.

Such, then, are the difficulties in determining the day of the crucifixion, and they may be summed up in the following manner. The first three Gospels say that it was after the Passover; the fourth says that it was before the Passover; and external historical testimony, as we have shown, decides in favour of the fourth. Again, of the two occasions for the preparation, which was on the same day that the crucifixion took place, Luke alone expressly says that it was on Friday. But if we neglect in Matthew and Mark the mention of the Passover and unleavened bread, those Gospels, as well as John, will be better understood by taking the preparation spoken of to be, not the Friday, but the Thursday evening, without considering for what it was a preparation.

On The Last Supper.

WE have thus seen that in the matter of the day of the week on which the Passover was eaten, the weight of evidence rests with the fourth Gospel, rather than with the three others. If we now examine the four accounts of dipping the sop and pointing out Judas as the traitor, we shall see that there also the fourth Gospel carries with it a greater

appearance of exactness. We read in John (xiii.
23), correcting the Authorized Version, " Now there
was lying at meat in Jesus's bosom one of his disciples whom Jesus loved. To him therefore Simon
Peter beckoned to ask who it was of whom he spake.
He then, leaning back on Jesus's breast, saith to
him, Lord, who is it? Jesus answereth, He it is
to whom I shall give the sop when I have dipped
it. And after dipping it he giveth it to Judas
Iscariot."

Thus John, the disciple whom Jesus loved, was
lying on that part of the couch which was said to be
in Jesus's bosom ; and he thought he was able, by
simply leaning back his head, to ask Peter's question
so quietly that the others should not hear it either
asked or answered. But Jesus, yet more cautious of
being heard, tells him that he will answer it by a
sign, namely by giving a sop to the suspected traitor. And he does so accordingly. Now if we read
this narrative in Matthew and Mark, we shall see no
reason whatever for Jesus pointing out the traitor by
a sign, rather than by naming him openly. Luke
does not mention the sign, or that any answer was
given to the question who would be the traitor ; his
narrative seems to be incomplete. But Matthew
and Mark, if incomplete, are faultily so ; they mention the sign of dipping into the dish, but fail to
explain to us why it was used. The fourth Gospel
alone does this, and thereby gains a claim to be
thought in this matter also more trustworthy than
the others.

On the Driving the Dealers out of the Temple-yard.

BEFORE attempting to form a chronological table of the ministry, which can be formed for the fourth Gospel only, we must consider one important passage in which John is contradicted by the three other evangelists. This is in the driving the dealers out of the temple-yard shortly before a Passover. John places this at the beginning of the ministry, and the others at the end. Here, I think, we may safely rely on Matthew, Mark, and Luke, and consider the passage in John (ii. 13—iii. 21) as being out of place, for the following reasons :

First, after this act and the conversation with Nicodemus in Jerusalem, we are told, iii. 22, that Jesus and his disciples go into Judea, which could hardly be said at that time when the division of the land into twelve tribes was forgotten, and the whole country was divided into Galilee, Samaria, and Judea. At that time Jerusalem was in Judea, and travellers could hardly be described as going from Jerusalem into Judea.

Secondly, the driving the dealers out of the court of the Gentiles, with the approval, which it must have had, of the surrounding multitude, was an act of such political importance, that we may well consider it as one of the reasons for the rulers wishing to have Jesus removed out of their way, as a popular teacher who was interfering with their authority. In the other Gospels this act naturally follows upon his triumphal entry into Jerusalem, with a crowd of believers who had accepted him as a prophet.

Thirdly, if this act and the Passover which is mentioned with it are allowed to stand in their present place, then the fourth Gospel mentions three Passovers as falling within the time of the ministry. This would require us to allow to it a space of more than two years; whereas we have seen reason to believe that the ministry was limited to one year and seven months.

For these reasons I think we may follow Matthew, Mark, and Luke, in thinking that the cleansing of the temple-yard did not take place sooner than a few days before the crucifixion. The removal of this act to a later part of the history will carry with it not only the conversation with Nicodemus, but the remark that it was already forty-six years from when Herod began to rebuild the temple. But this remark is rather tantalizing than important; for Josephus leaves us so far in doubt about the exact year in which Herod began to build that we cannot count from it with any certainty.

Of our four histories of the ministry, Matthew, Mark, and Luke give no hint of the time of year in which any event happens, except in the case of the crucifixion, and of one other event, which we see was at the time of the harvest. But John has many such hints, besides mentioning the occasion of six Jewish feasts. By the help of these we may form a chronological table of the ministry, at least for the fourth Gospel. For determining the time occupied by the events in the other Gospels we have no such helps; and we shall confine ourselves to the fourth Gospel, making no use of the others except for two particulars. First, we shall borrow from Luke that the baptism took place in the fifteenth year of Tiberius ; and we shall be guided, as we have said, by the three Synoptics, as they are sometimes called, in considering Christ's driving the dealers out of the temple-yard as having happened on this last visit to Jerusalem, and in thinking the passage, John ii. 13—iii. 21, out of its proper place, and in thus reducing the number of feasts mentioned to five.

TABLE OF CHRONOLOGY OF CHRIST'S MINISTRY.

A.D. 27.

Aug. 29. New-year's Day, and the first day of the fifteenth year of Tiberius. Soon afterwards Jesus is baptized by John, Luke iii. 1.

> [*Note.* The visit to Jerusalem and cleansing the temple-yard at the Passover of John ii. 13—iii. 21, belong to the last Passover.]

Oct. John is baptizing in Ænon, John iii. 23, probably before the rains in November, when the crowds could not be abroad. Jesus goes into Judea.

Dec. There are yet four months to the harvest, which was to begin in April, John iv. 35. He is in Samaria, at Jacob's Well.

Dec. There was a feast of the Jews, probably the Dedication, John v. 1. Jesus goes to Jerusalem.

A.D. 28.

Mar. The Passover is at hand, John vi. 4. Jesus is beyond the Lake of Galilee.

> [*Note.* Between John vi. 4 and vii. 1, the events of six months are passed over unmen-

A.D. 28

tioned. They are described in the other Gospels, and assigned to this space of time by the
mention of the wheat harvest, which is in
May.   See Matthew xii. 1 ; Mark ii. 23 ; Luke
vi. 1.]

Sept.   Now the Jews' Feast of Tabernacles was
             at hand, John vii. 1. Jesus goes to
             Jerusalem from Galilee.

Dec.   Jesus is still in Jerusalem at the Feast of
             Dedication, John x. 22.

A.D. 29.

April   2. The moon was new at Jerusalem on
           Saturday, one hour after sunset, accord-
           ing to Professor Adams and Mr. Hind.

April   3. This is the first day of the month Nisan,
           being the day of the new moon.

April 10. Jesus arrives in Bethany six days before
          the ˉPassover, John xii. 1.   This is a
          Sunday.

          In this week he drives the dealers out of
          the temple-yard.   This was forty-six
          years and some months after Herod
          began to rebuild the temple, John ii.
          20.   According to Matthew, Mark, and
          Luke, this was on his last visit to
          Jerusalem.

April 14. On Thursday Jesus is crucified at noon.
          It is the day of the preparation for the
          Passover, John xix. 14.   This is the
          12th day of Nisan.

April 14. On Thursday evening after sunset was the
          preparation, or ceremonial search for
          leaven.   Not twenty-three hours before
          the Passover, as usual, because that

would have been during the Sabbath ;
but a day and twenty-three hours before,
as the Passover was to be eaten on
Saturday evening. See the Mishna.
During the night Joseph and Nicodemus
embalm and bury Jesus, John xix. 38.

April **15.** No event of Friday during the daylight is
here mentioned. See Matt. xxvii. **62,**
where the obtaining the guard and sealing the tomb belong to this day.

April **15.** At sunset on Friday the Sabbath begins,
when neither the preparation nor the
purchase of the cloth nor embalmment
could have taken place.

April **16.** Saturday the **14**th day of Nisan, when the
Passover is eaten in the evening.

April **17.** On Sunday, the first day of the week, the
disciples find the tomb empty, John xx. **1.**
It is three full days, wanting only six
hours, from the crucifixion on Thursday.

On the Year of Jesus's Birth.

For this date we have no other authority than the
words of Luke, in chap. iii. 23, " And Jesus when
he began "—that is, when he began his ministry—
" was about thirty years of age." These words do
not purport to give us great exactness, and they may
be founded on the known requirements of the Levi-
tical law, which fixed upon thirty as the age when
the priests entered on their service. See Numbers
iv. **2,** and 1 Chron. xxiii. **3,** where only men of thirty

years of age and upward are registered for the priesthood. However, if we are to build upon these words of Luke as being exact, we should place the birth of Jesus in the autumn of the year B.C. 4. This would make him thirty years old when he stood up to read the Scriptures in the synagogue at Nazareth, soon after September, A.D. 27.

Hence we learn that our vulgar era has been fixed four years wrong. This mistake was made by Dionysius Exiguus, who wrote on the Calendar of the Church, and declared the well-known year of the consulship of Philoxenus and Probus, the third indiction in the reign of the Emperor Justin, to be the year of our Lord 525. His opinion was accepted by the Church, and, consequently, by the later writers, who used the birth of Christ as a date; and all Christendom have counted the years forward from that year to the present in obedience to the calculation of Dionysius Exiguus, whose mistake leads to no error in chronology.

Woodfall and Kinder, Printers, Milford Lane, Strand, W.C

ND - #0036 - 261022 - C0 - 229/152/4 [6] - CB - 9780265220948 - Gloss Lamination